Patrick **Roy**

ANDREW PODNIEKS

GREYSTONE BOOKS

Douglas & McIntyre

Vancouver/Toronto

Greystone Books
A division of Douglas & McIntyre Ltd.
1615 Venables Street
Vancouver, British Columbia
Canada v5l 2h1

Canadian Cataloguing in Publication Data
Podnieks, Andrew.
    Patrick Roy
    (Hockey heroes)
    ISBN 1-55054-641-4

    1. Roy, Patrick—Juvenile literature. 2 Hockey goalkeepers—Canada—
Biography—Juvenile literature. I. Title. II. Series.
GV848.5.R69P62 1998   j796.962'092   c98-910271-8

Editing by Michael Carroll
Cover and text design by Peter Cocking
Front cover photograph by John Giamundo/Bruce Bennett Studios
Back cover photograph by Wen Roberts/Bruce Bennett Studios
Printed and bound in Canada by Friesens
Printed on acid-free paper ∞

The publisher gratefully acknowledges the assistance of the Canada Council for the Arts and of the British Columbia Ministry of Tourism, Small Business and Culture. The publisher also acknowledges the financial support of the Government of Canada through the Book Publishing Industry Development Program for its publishing activities.

Patrick is one of the most skilled goalies in the NHL. Like most players, though, his dream began when he was a boy.

CHAPTER ONE

Beginnings

By the time Patrick Roy was seven years old, he was obsessed with playing road hockey with his friends. They only had a rubber ball and a net, but that was all the boys needed. Because he was the smallest, Patrick always played goal. On Saturday nights he would watch *Hockey Night in Canada* and use pillows as pads while playing goal in the house. He dreamed of playing in the Montreal Forum, and often pretended he was Ken Dryden or another famous Montreal Canadien goalie.

Patrick was born in Sainte-Foy, a wealthy area of Quebec City, Quebec. When growing up, Patrick's father, Michel, loved tennis and baseball. When Patrick's mother was young, she was a top-ranked synchronized swimmer. Athletics and fitness have always been important in the Roy family.

Patrick has a sister and a brother, and while they were kids, Patrick was obsessed with one thing—being a goalie. His heroes were Rogatien Vachon of the Los Angeles Kings and Daniel Bouchard of the Atlanta Flames (now in Calgary). Once, Patrick even met Daniel Bouchard, who gave Patrick his goal stick. That stick meant the world to the young boy. Every night after that, when Patrick went to bed, he slept with the stick that his hero had given him. He felt that if he could hold that stick and dream of being an NHL goalie, one day that dream might come true.

At the age of 17, Patrick decided not to attend grade 11 high school. This was a big decision. Everyone knows how important an education is to becoming successful. But Patrick's parents supported him all the way. Patrick had played well as a midget for the Sainte-Foy Gouverneurs and knew he could play in the NHL. Instead of school, he went to the training camp of the Granby Bisons of the Quebec Major Junior Hockey League (QMJHL).

Patrick keeps his job simple: just get in front of the puck.

One of the reasons Patrick ranks among the best goalies in the world is because of the three years he spent at Granby. He played on a terrible hockey team and on average allowed five

goals a game. That's not a good average at all. But the only way a goalie can improve is to keep playing. Patrick faced 40 to 50 shots every night from the world's best juniors in the Quebec League. He didn't mind. He knew the practice would be good for him in the long run.

Just think, in his first season in Granby, 1982–83, his goals-against average (GAA) was 6.26. In his second year it was 4.44. The GAA is the average number of goals allowed by a goalie per game over the course of a season. So, even though these weren't good averages, the Montreal Canadiens could see that Patrick was talented. In the summer of 1984, the Canadiens used their fourth-round selection in the NHL Entry Draft to call the name "Patrick Roy."

After the draft, Patrick played most of the next season with Granby. But he also played his first professional game in the NHL. There was a bit of luck involved. He was called up by Montreal mostly to watch the Canadiens and to see what it was like to play in the NHL. But on the night of February 23, 1985, he dressed as backup goalie to starter Doug Soetaert in a game

THE PATRICK ROY FILE

Position: Goaltender

Born: October 5, 1965, Sainte-Foy, Quebec

Height: Six feet (1.83 meters)

Weight: 192 pounds (87 kilograms)

Catches: Left

Number: 33

Nicknames: Saint Patrick, Goose

Favorite Food: Steak

Motto: Never give up

Off-Season Hobby: Golf

Childhood Hockey Heroes:
Daniel Bouchard, Rogatien Vachon

Hockey Highlight:
The 1993 Stanley Cup playoffs

against the Winnipeg Jets (now the Phoenix Coyotes). Over the first two periods, Soetaert didn't play well at all. He let in three easy goals in the second period. Coach Jacques Lemaire decided to put Patrick in net to start the third period. The score was tied 4–4, but Montreal scored twice and Patrick didn't allow a goal. Just like that, Patrick won the first game he ever played in the NHL. It was a dream come true.

Soon after that, Montreal sent Patrick to the Sherbrooke Canadiens, Montreal's American Hockey League (AHL) farm team. This was where the young stars gained experience and became familiar with pro hockey. Patrick didn't think he was going to play much because the Junior Canadiens already had two goalies. They didn't need another. But luck was on Patrick's side again. One night, near the end of the season, Patrick dressed as backup goalie. In the early part of the game, the starting goalie had equipment troubles. He was forced to leave the ice for a short time. Patrick took his place in the net, and the starting goalie never played again that season.

Patrick so impressed his Granby coach, Pierre Creamer, that he played the rest of the game. He then became the starting goalie for Sherbrooke in the playoffs. Patrick was incredible. He won 10 of 13

Practice Makes Perfect

Playing on a bad team might mean losing a lot of games, but it is never something you should hate. There is always something good to come out of losing, as Patrick Roy found out. "It was tough playing for them," he admitted later about his three years in Granby. "But I got a lot of work and it was a good experience. I learned to deal with the frustrations of losing and now I appreciate more the enjoyment of winning."

games and kept his goals-against average an amazing 2.89. The team won the Calder Cup, which is like the Stanley Cup for the AHL. "He's probably the main reason they won the championship," Montreal head coach Jean Perron said. "They weren't the best team during the season, but he kept making save after save in the playoffs. He was always in control. After watching him in Sherbrooke, I knew he could play for the Canadiens."

With those words, Patrick Roy's days in Granby were over. His short career as a minor pro in Sherbrooke had also ended. His dream life as a member of the Montreal Canadiens of the National Hockey League was about to begin.

Patrick learned quickly

that having excellent

body control is vital to

being successful. Even

when he's down, Patrick's

legs are spread out.

CHAPTER TWO

Sensational Rookie

Becoming a goalie for the Montreal Canadiens isn't as simple as strapping on the equipment and making the saves. It all has to do with tradition. Montreal has won 24 Stanley Cups, the most of any team ever. In Montreal the team has had some of the greatest goalies to play the game: Georges Vézina (after whom the most valuable goalie trophy is named), George Hainsworth, Bill Durnan, Jacques Plante, Gump Worsley and, more recently, Ken Dryden in the 1970s.

So, when you play in Montreal, you are expected to play the position as well as Georges Vézina and all the other greats.

During his brief stay in Sherbrooke, Patrick met goalie coach François Allaire. The two men liked each other instantly and were in perfect agreement about how to approach the game. They felt a goalie could play the position in a different, yet successful, way. Allaire could see that Patrick's reflexes were amazing. But he didn't always have his body properly positioned. Patrick liked to go down to make a save. Allaire wanted to teach Patrick *how* to go down. Patrick had to be aware that if he did it properly it could be used to stop shooters better than any other style. Allaire taught Patrick everything about playing goal.

When Patrick got to Montreal's training camp in 1985, it was his first time trying out with an NHL team. Because he was a rookie, he was considered to be the third best goalie on the Canadiens after Steve Penney and Doug Soetaert. This put him in a tough position because most teams only need two goalies during the year. Soon the season was about to begin. Montreal general manager John Ferguson told coach Jean Perron that Patrick had to be sent to the minors. But the coach said, "No way. I can live with three goaltenders." Patrick was that good. And besides, Steve Penney was injured.

Junk Food

While playing in Sherbrooke, Patrick Roy was nicknamed "Humpty Dumpty" by his teammates because of his love for potato chips. When he got to Montreal, the players called him *casseau*. This is a French word for the cardboard container used to serve french fries. Montreal coach Jean Perron admitted that Patrick's diet was a real concern: "He lacked energy early in the season and much of it had to do with the food he was eating."

Patrick started the first game that season and won 5–3
in Pittsburgh. When Penney was healthy again, the coach put
him back in the net and Patrick had to sit on the bench. But
Perron was never happy with the way Steve Penney played:
"I didn't like Penney's style, didn't like his trapper glove. He
couldn't grab the puck. Every time I started him, I didn't have
confidence. Soetaert was hot and cold. I started putting Patrick
into tough situations, especially on the road.... Even in practice I could see he was so much better than the other two guys."

Patrick's rise to number-one goalie of the Canadiens was
fast. But staying on top wasn't so simple. First, NHL games
are a lot more physically demanding than junior or AHL games.
For example, Patrick is six feet (1.83 meters) tall, but back
then weighed only 165 pounds (75 kilograms). He lacked
strength when he became an NHL regular. The team actually
had to hire someone to teach Patrick
about what foods he should eat.
The most important are whole-grain
cereals and bread, fruits and vege-
tables, especially beans and peas.
These foods are rich in vitamins
and minerals and help build your
strength. The team also told him
to drink plenty of water during
games. Every chance he got, Patrick
was supposed to drink water to
improve his stamina.

Early in his first season, Patrick played inconsistently. He would make a series of great saves, then let in a long shot from outside the blueline. He would keep his team in the game, then go down early and let an easy shot sail over his arm into the net. Some teammates wanted coach Perron to play Steve Penney instead. The hometown crowd cheered Patrick's great saves but also booed his mistakes.

One of Patrick's greatest strengths during his first NHL season was his ability to handle the pressures off the ice. He took criticism well. He welcomed the challenge of being the number-one man when so many people said he wasn't good enough. As the year went along, his diet improved and he gained strength and weight. The team started to have confidence in him. He became a goalie other teams began to respect and then fear.

Hockey Night in Canada television commentator and former NHL goalie Greg Millen talked about what effect Patrick's great season had on the rest of the league: "There used to be a feeling that goalies did not mature until they were 25 or 26 years of age. It's my opinion that Roy changed that outlook. Here was a young guy who gets drafted by the Canadiens in 1984 and takes over almost immediately." Patrick ended the year with a record of 23–18–3 (wins-losses-ties) and a GAA of 3.35 a game. His impressive regular season was over, but it was time for the greatest challenge of them all—the Stanley Cup playoffs.

> In his first year, Patrick let in a few goals he should have stopped.

There is no greater

accomplishment in hockey

than skating around the

ice with the Stanley Cup.

Patrick did that his very

first year in Montreal.

CHAPTER THREE

The First Stanley Cup

"He loves a challenge," Montreal coach Jean Perron said about Patrick in 1986. "He says to me, 'The more pressure there is, the better I like it.'" The Canadiens finished the 1985–86 regular season with a record of 40–33–7 (wins-losses-ties). This put them in second place in their division behind the Quebec Nordiques (now the Colorado Avalanche).

Montreal faced the Boston Bruins in the first round of the playoffs in a best three-of-five series. The Canadiens won the series easily, by scores of 3–1 and 3–2 at the Forum in Montreal, and 4–3 in the Boston Garden. Patrick played every minute and allowed just six goals. In the division finals, Montreal played the Hartford Whalers (now the Carolina Hurricanes). This was a best-of-seven series. It turned out to be quite a battle, but the Canadiens finally won on Claude Lemieux's overtime goal in Game 7. They were now in the conference championships playing the New York Rangers.

By this point, there were only two other teams besides New York and Montreal that could win the Stanley Cup—the St. Louis Blues and the Calgary Flames. But Patrick and the Canadiens were the focus of attention, and number 33 couldn't have been happier. He said that being in a big game didn't make him scared. It made him play *better*. "The more I played, the more confidence I got," he told reporters. "When they decided to play me in the playoffs, my confidence grew even more."

The Butterfly

It was with the help of François Allaire that Patrick Roy developed his butterfly style of goalkeeping. Patrick falls to his knees, spreads his arms slightly, and covers as much of the lower half of the net as he can with his body *(see photo on page 18)*. Allaire explains: "Nowadays players don't have two or three seconds to shoot and to score up top. That's why the bottom of the net is so important for the goalie."

Patrick has often talked about the dreams he has the night before a game. Dreams are important in building confidence. They make you feel that anything is possible, just like all those years ago when Patrick slept with Daniel Bouchard's goal stick... and dreamed of playing in the NHL. Dreams always help Patrick play better: "I sleep well and I try to dream about what is going to happen

PATRICK'S GREATEST GAME

Patrick Roy believes he played his best game ever during the 1986 Stanley Cup playoffs against the New York Rangers. The Montreal Canadiens had won the first two games of the series at the Forum and played Game 3 at Madison Square Garden. The Canadiens won 4–3 in overtime. Patrick said, "I felt like a wall, honestly. Like nothing is going to stop our game. Kind of like in the zone." After winning the Stanley Cup, Patrick was awarded the Conn Smythe Trophy as the best player in the playoffs.

in the game—where they drop the puck, if they shoot. . . . You have to be cocky to be a goaltender, but cocky on a good side. You have to tell yourself you can do a good job."

Eventually Patrick's fans found out about his weird on-ice conversations. "I talk to my goalposts," he admitted. "It's a superstition. The forwards talk to each other. The defense is always close, but a goaltender is alone."

Patrick's "talks" sound kind of funny, but they've always helped him. Here's what he does. Just before the start of each game, he skates out of his net about halfway to the blueline. He turns around and stares at the net. That's when he talks to his posts. He says the longer he stares at the net, the smaller it looks. This helps give him even more confidence. "They're my friends. They listen," he insists, trying to explain his strange habit.

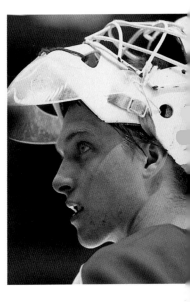

When he talks to the posts, do they say anything back? Yes, he replies. They say, *"Ping,"* which is French for "bang."

The Canadiens won both home games against the Rangers by scores of 2–1 and 6–2. While Patrick and Montreal played very well, the Rangers weren't as strong as they had been during the year. Before Game 3, New York forward Wilf Paiement did what no player should do—he challenged the other team. He said about Patrick's performance in the first two games: "Anyone can make 20 saves. Let's see what he can do with 40 shots."

Sure enough, New York fired 47 shots at Patrick in Game 3. Unfortunately for the Broadway Blueshirts (as the Rangers are sometimes called), Patrick stopped 44 of them and Montreal won the game 4–3. His goalie opponent at the other end praised Patrick's effort: "It was one of the best goaltending games I've ever opposed," said John Vanbiesbrouck, one of the game's greatest goalies himself.

The Rangers won Game 4 at Madison Square Garden in New York. But then Montreal eliminated them two nights later and moved on to the Stanley Cup finals to meet the Calgary Flames. Patrick gave up five goals in Game 1 against the Flames, the most he had given up in the playoffs. After that, he was beaten only eight more times in the last four games, all Montreal wins. The Canadiens had won the Stanley Cup!

Patrick played all 20 games for the Canadiens in the 1986 playoffs, winning 15 of them. He won the Stanley Cup in his first year with the team. He was also the youngest player ever to be awarded the Conn Smythe Trophy, which is given each year to the best player in the playoffs. Not bad for a rookie. After the game, the Canadiens flew home from Calgary and arrived in Montreal at 6:30 in the morning in heavy fog where a crowd of 10,000 fans waited to greet them.

In the 1986 playoffs Patrick won the Conn Smythe Trophy.

Patrick was now the most famous person in Montreal. He was French Canadian. He was playing the most important position on the Montreal Canadiens. He was young and had already won the Stanley Cup. He was a hero.

In the 1993 playoffs, Patrick

seemed to fill the whole

net. He won 16 of 20

games and led Montreal to

a second Stanley Cup.

CHAPTER FOUR

Winning the Cup Again

The Canadiens had an amazing "dynasty" when they won four Stanley Cups in a row from 1976 to 1980. Since then, though, they hadn't done very well. Without Patrick the previous year, they likely wouldn't have won, either.

At the start of the 1986–87 season, people assumed that Patrick could win every game himself. He'd have to. There wasn't much scoring on the team and the defense was weak. Reality soon caught up with expectations. Patrick had a good record of 22–16–6 and a GAA of 2.93. The Canadiens made it to the

semifinals in the playoffs, but they were crushed by the Philadel-
phia Flyers in six games. Patrick gave up 22 goals in the series
and was unable to prevent the awesome Flyers from taking
advantage of Montreal's weaknesses. The long season was over.

The Canadiens continued to play good, but not great, hockey.
It was always Patrick who kept the team competitive. They went
to the finals again in 1989 but lost to the Calgary Flames, the
same team Montreal had beaten in 1986. In the next three
years, they lost in the second round of the playoffs each time.

In December 1992, Patrick was 27 years old and in his
eighth full season with the Canadiens. Despite all he had done
for Montreal, there were rumors he was going to be traded.
A French-language radio talk show conducted a survey with its
listeners. Everyone seemed to agree it was time to trade "Saint
Patrick," as the fans called him. The trade never happened,
but the rumors made Patrick play even better. He
finished the season with a respectable 3.20 GAA.

Patrick stops Calgary

sharpshooter Theoren

Fleury on this rush.

As in 1986, most people around the league
were looking at the obvious teams to win the
Stanley Cup in the spring of 1993. Pittsburgh
still had Mario Lemieux and had won an amazing
56 games. Boston and Quebec finished ahead of
Montreal in the Adams Division. Chicago and Detroit had more
than 100 points in the Norris Division. Vancouver was a team
full of hope and promise. The Maple Leafs were one of the best
teams in the second half of the season after acquiring Doug
Gilmour from the Flames early in the new year.

SUPERSTITIONS

Like most goalies, Patrick Roy has many superstitions to help him play well. On the day of a game, he always eats spaghetti and drinks water at 1:00 p.m. After warming up just before a game, he bounces the same puck in the same way in the dressing room. Before going out on the ice, he writes the name of his children on his game stick.

When he's on the ice, he never skates on the red and blue lines. While playing, he snaps his head from side to side, which is why one of his nicknames is "Goose." Watch how he flicks his stick from post to post. Notice how he skates circles in the corners during whistles. It's all part of his routine that makes him more comfortable and confident in goal.

But Patrick was on a mission. In the opening-round series, the Canadiens squeaked by their provincial rivals, the Quebec Nordiques, four games to two. Four of the games were won by one goal and three were decided in sudden-death overtime. In the next round, they beat Buffalo four straight. Amazingly, though, all four games in the Montreal sweep were identical 4–3 scores (and again three went into overtime). That's never happened before.

In 1993 the NHL was divided into two conferences, the Prince of Wales and the Clarence Campbell. In the Prince of Wales Conference finals, Montreal played the New York Islanders. The Islanders had done Montreal a huge favor by eliminating the mighty Pittsburgh Penguins in seven games. Unfortunately, when they entered Montreal, they were a tired team that was easy to beat. The Canadiens had little challenge. They won in five games, two of which went into overtime. In this series, Patrick gave up just 11 goals. And just as in 1986, Montreal was in the finals almost by some sort of miracle.

St. Louis had stunned Chicago in the first round, and Los Angeles had eliminated Vancouver in one of the Clarence Campbell semifinals. The Los Angeles Kings were taken to seven games by Toronto, the surprise in these playoffs. But the Leafs lost thanks to some bad luck in Game 6 and a heroic performance from the Great One, Wayne Gretzky, in Game 7.

But like the Islanders in the semifinals, the Kings had used all their energy just to get to where they were. Los Angeles had played 19 games by this time, Montreal just 15. The Canadiens were more rested and physically better prepared to perform well in the finals.

And besides, they had Patrick Roy in net.

Nowadays it is simply called the "wink." It was just one moment in the finals by Saint Patrick, but it is thought by many to have given the Habs (as Montreal is often called) a huge mental advantage that helped decide the Stanley Cup. It was Game 4 in Los Angeles. The Kings trailed the series 2–1, and the game was tied in the third period. Overtime seemed a sure thing. By this time in the playoffs, however, the Habs had won an incredible nine overtime games in a row. Obviously Los Angeles didn't want to see this match go into overtime, as well. They were that afraid of Patrick, who had an overtime shutout streak of more than 90 minutes.

In 1993 Patrick won 10 straight overtime playoff games.

Midway through the period, Patrick smothered the puck and the Kings' Tomas Sandstrom skated in, hoping for a rebound. The whistle blew, and Patrick looked up at Sandstrom and winked at him. Television cameras caught the moment and played it over and over as the most important incident in the playoffs.

Some people watching the game on television thought the wink was an act of overconfidence and disrespect, but Patrick disagreed: "I knew Sandstrom was taking lots of shots, but not getting anything. And I knew he wasn't going to beat me...."

I wasn't being arrogant. I was just in the 'zone.'" Patrick was in the zone the whole playoffs, that feeling you have when you think you can stop anything. Nothing is going to beat you when you're in the zone. In these 1993 playoffs, Patrick won an NHL record 10 overtime games in a row.

Overall, in the playoffs, Patrick had a sensational 16–4 record with an excellent goals-against average of 2.13. His overtime winning streak lasted 96 minutes and 39 seconds. Without any other possible choice, the league awarded him his second Conn Smythe Trophy. Patrick was only the second goalie to win the honor a second time. The other man was Hockey Hall of Fame legend Bernie Parent.

Hockey, like life, is unpredictable. Patrick won two Stanley Cups with teams barely talented enough to make the playoffs. The next season the team looked like one of the strongest in the league but lost in the first round of the playoffs. The Canadiens finished with a 41–29–14 record, and Patrick was in net for 35 of their 41 wins. He had signed a huge contract at the beginning of the year that made him the third-highest-paid player in the league. Only Mario Lemieux and Eric Lindros earned more. This was a remarkable reward for a goaltender. Patrick couldn't have been happier. "The most important thing," he said after signing the four-year deal, "is to have the chance to finish my career in Montreal."

However, the day after Game 2 of the Canadiens' first-round match against Boston, disaster struck in a strange way. With

> When Patrick plays at the top of the crease, he's in control.

the series tied one game all, Patrick suffered an attack of appendicitis. He was taken to Montreal General Hospital, but every effort was made by the doctors not to operate. This was very unusual because appendicitis almost always meant surgery. But an operation required at least two months' recovery time. Patrick would have missed the rest of the year with the team.

Instead, the doctors gave him special drugs to help his appendix. While he lay in his hospital bed, Montreal had to play Game 3 of their series against the Bruins. Backup goalie Ron Tugnutt didn't play well in goal that game. Boston beat Montreal 6–3 to take a 2–1 lead in the series.

Patrick was determined. He said he felt good enough to play. His appendix had returned to normal, and the team needed him. On the morning of Game 4, he checked out of the hospital. That night he stopped 39 shots to lead the Habs to a 5–2 victory that tied the series. The Bruins went on to win the matchup in seven games, but Patrick's heroic effort in playing the final four games was truly courageous.

PATRICK'S EQUIPMENT

One mental and physical advantage that Patrick Roy has always had over shooters is his equipment. The NHL rules say the legal width for pads is 12 inches (30 centimeters). Most players believe Patrick's pads are much wider. Patrick is also accused of wearing a very "droopy" sweater, which hangs below his armpits to fill spaces. His shoulder pads are also oversized, and he has extra padding at the top of his pants. Regarding what the NHL permits in equipment, former Calgary goalie Rick Wamsley once said that, "Patrick's 'gray area' is blacker than most." But as Patrick has pointed out, he has been checked by the league and never been fined. At least he has the other team thinking!

CHAPTER FIVE

A New Team

The 1994–95 season was Patrick's worst with the Canadiens. For the first and only time in his career, he had a losing record (17 wins, 20 losses and six ties). Montreal failed to make the playoffs for the first time since 1970. By the time the next season started, things didn't look good for the famous club. From the team that won the Stanley Cup two years before in 1993, only four players remained. The general manager, coach, assistant coaches and head scout had also been fired and replaced. The club that once prided itself on tradition now looked weak in this respect.

The night of December 2, 1995, may be the lowest moment in the history of the Montreal hockey club. It is certainly the lowest point of Patrick's career. The Habs played Detroit at home that night. The Red Wings were an awesome team, a Stanley Cup favorite. They played to kill. In the first period, Detroit scored five goals, but Montreal coach Mario Tremblay kept Patrick in the game to start the second period. This was unusual. Most times, when a star goalie has such a bad start, he is replaced. But Patrick wasn't, and the Red Wings didn't let up.

The fans began to boo Patrick terribly every time he touched the puck or made a routine save. With the score 8–1, Patrick made a simple play. The fans cheered insultingly, and Patrick raised both his arms as if he had won the Stanley Cup. He was just as insulting right back. It wasn't until the score was 9–1 that coach Mario Tremblay took Patrick out of the game. As Patrick skated off the ice, he walked past the coach. He stopped to talk to team president Ronald Corey, who always sat directly behind the players' bench. He told Corey he had played his last game as a member of the Montreal Canadiens. He meant it.

Patrick sits in shock after being beaten by Detroit nine times.

Right after the game, the Canadiens suspended Patrick. But the terrible events of that evening weren't a surprise to Patrick's teammates. Coach Tremblay and his number-one goalie didn't get along and had fought many times before. But for the coach to leave an All-Star goalie in a lopsided game like that was really the wrong thing

to do. It was doubly strange because Tremblay and Patrick had been roommates on road trips during Patrick's rookie season when Tremblay was still a player.

Four days later, Patrick was traded to the Colorado Avalanche, along with team captain Mike Keane, for young goalie Jocelyn Thibault and wingers Martin Rucinsky and Andrei Kovalenko. Patrick's career with the Montreal Canadiens was over. His contract that was supposed to last the rest of his career in Montreal was now transferred to Denver, Colorado.

The Colorado Avalanche used to be the Quebec Nordiques. The team had moved from Quebec City to Denver just before the start of 1995–96 season. Therefore, this was still very much a French-Canadian team. If the Nordiques had still been

playing in Quebec City, Montreal would never have traded their superstar to their provincial rival. For Patrick, who was born just outside Quebec City, being traded to Colorado was a bit like coming home. There was no other team he would have been happier playing for.

Patrick's first game with the Avalanche wasn't very good. He lost 5–3 to Edmonton. "I can't say this was my best game," he admitted afterward. "My legs were a little tired. . . . I just have to make some adjustments. I'll take a day off and get some work in practice and regroup from there." And that's exactly what he did.

When Patrick faced his old Montreal mates later in the season, he stopped 37 shots to help his new Colorado team win 5–2. "I think every athlete has pride," he said. "When you face your ex-team, you always want to do well. You want to show that your new team made a good deal to get you." In April Montreal was knocked out in the first round of the playoffs. There were no cheers of "Saint Jocelyn" for their young new goalie Jocelyn Thibault. Patrick Roy's playoff performance in Colorado, though, was another story.

Unlike in Montreal, Patrick had plenty of talent on the team in Colorado. Also, he was experienced enough to know how to fit in. "When you get traded, like what happened to me where you played in a big place like Montreal and were the leader of the team, it puts a lot of attention on yourself. When you come to a team where Joe Sakic, Peter Forsberg and Claude Lemieux are playing, they are the big attractions of the team. You try to fit and don't try to change the routine of the other guys. Sometimes when you are used to something else, that's the toughest part of the adjustment.

Colorado Honors Patrick

The night of February 23, 1996, will always be special for Patrick Roy. He had won his 300th career game four nights earlier against Edmonton. On this night, the Avalanche gave him a very special honor in a pregame ceremony before playing the Los Angeles Kings. Artist Denny Dent set up a large canvas in one corner of the rink, and Patrick posed for him in the net. Dent painted the quick portrait in just 10 minutes. Then Patrick watched the game from the bench as backup goalie Stephane Fiset helped beat Los Angeles 6–2.

But to me, it came pretty easy and the guys helped me out a lot. They are really good guys."

In the 1996 playoffs, Patrick made Colorado look good and Montreal bad for trading him. The Avalanche won the Stanley Cup. They won because they had such tremendous talent. They had four strong forward lines, six solid defensemen and a great goaltender. Patrick played all but one minute of the 22 playoff games. He had an incredible record of 16 wins and only six losses, with a superb 2.10 goals-against average.

Colorado began the playoffs by beating Vancouver in six games, then eliminated Chicago in the next round in six games, as well. This set up a conference final with the Red Wings, the same team that had scored nine goals on Patrick in 30 minutes during his last night in goal for Montreal. But after watching Patrick give up just 14 goals in six games to his Chicago team, coach Craig Hartsburg knew Detroit wasn't good enough to beat Colorado: "Of the four goalies left in the playoffs, Colorado's is the best.... When Roy needs to, he simply shuts the door on you."

When Patrick is at the top of his game, he's unbeatable.

Patrick was once again a key to Colorado's victory over Detroit. Leading two games to one, the Avs (their nickname) were in Detroit. In the previous match, Patrick had experienced his worst performance of the playoffs, letting in six goals. He predicted he'd play better in Game 4, and he did. Early in the contest, he stopped Kris Draper on a breakaway. That was the turning

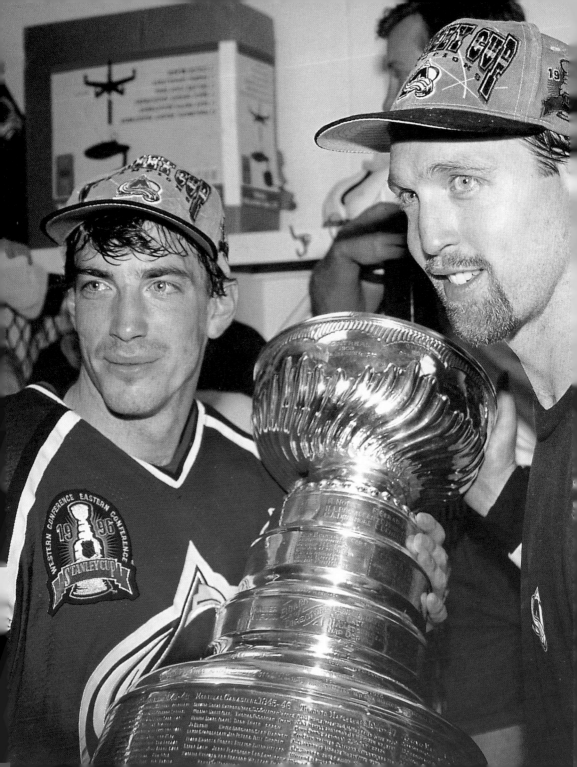

point of the game, and Colorado won 4–2 to take a 3–1 series lead. The Avs never looked back and advanced to the finals by eliminating the Wings in six games. After that they swept the Florida Panthers in four games. Patrick had won his third Stanley Cup, his first with his new team.

The following year, in the spring of 1997, the Red Wings eliminated Colorado from the playoffs and went on to win the Stanley Cup themselves. Patrick, though, became the all-time NHL goalie leader in playoff victories, games and minutes. Then, in February 1998, Patrick played in his first international hockey tournament. He represented Canada at the Winter Olympics in Nagano, Japan. Although Canada didn't get a medal, Patrick won four games, shut out the Belarus team and recorded an excellent GAA of 1.46 in six games.

Patrick Roy has never been simple. He has never been easy to figure out, and never done things the easy way. One thing you can't argue, though. Wherever he has played, Patrick Roy has been a winner.

IT'S A TEAM GAME

"I never saw a guy lead a team by himself," Patrick Roy said about his first playoffs with Joe Sakic *(at left in facing photo)* and the rest of the Colorado Avalanche. "Even when I won the Conn Smythe Trophy in 1993, I didn't do it alone. There were lots of leaders on the team and players who made the difference in certain games. Every night it was a different player for us. This year is the same way. Joe is the leader on the ice, but the goalie has to make the save. He needs the defensemen to be sharp and the forwards to do their jobs. Joe is playing extremely well. But we also have Peter Forsberg, who is outstanding with Claude Lemieux and Valeri Kamensky."

STATISTICS

Quebec Major Junior Hockey League (QMJHL)
Regular Season

Year	Team	GP	W	L	T	SO	GAA
1982–83	Granby	54	13	35	1	0	6.26
1983–84	Granby	61	29	29	1	0	4.44
1984–85	Granby	44	16	25	1	0	5.55
Totals		**159**	**58**	**89**	**3**	**0**	**5.33**

Playoffs

Year	Team	GP	W	L	T	SO	GAA
1983–84	Granby	4	0	4	0	0	5.41

American Hockey League (AHL)
Regular Season

Year	Team	GP	W	L	T	SO	GAA
1984–85	Sherbrooke	1	1	0	0	0	4.00

Playoffs

Year	Team	GP	W	L	T	SO	GAA
1984–85	Sherbrooke	13	10	3	0	0	2.89

National Hockey League (NHL)
Regular Season

Year	Team	GP	W	L	T	SO	GAA
1984–85	Montreal	1	1	0	0	0	0.00
1985–86	Montreal	47	23	18	3	1	3.35
1986–87	Montreal	46	22	16	6	1	2.93
1987–88	Montreal	45	23	12	9	3	2.90
1988–89	Montreal	48	33	5	6	4	2.47
1989–90	Montreal	54	31	16	5	3	2.53
1990–91	Montreal	48	25	15	6	1	2.71
1991–92	Montreal	67	36	22	8	5	2.36
1992–93	Montreal	62	31	25	5	2	3.20
1993–94	Montreal	68	35	17	11	7	2.50
1994–95	Montreal	43	17	20	6	1	2.97
1995–96	Montreal	22	12	9	1	1	2.95
	Colorado	39	22	15	1	1	2.68
1996–97	Colorado	62	38	15	7	7	2.32
1997–98	Colorado	65	31	19	13	4	2.39
Totals		**717**	**380**	**224**	**87**	**41**	**2.69**

Playoffs

Year	Team	GP	W	L	SO	GAA
1985	Montreal	Did Not Play				
1986	Montreal	20	15	5	1	1.92
1987	Montreal	6	4	2	0	4.00
1988	Montreal	8	3	4	0	3.35
1989	Montreal	19	13	6	2	2.09
1990	Montreal	11	5	6	1	2.43
1991	Montreal	13	7	5	0	3.06
1992	Montreal	11	4	7	1	2.62
1993	Montreal	20	16	4	0	2.13
1994	Montreal	6	3	3	0	2.56
1995	Montreal	Did Not Qualify				
1996	Colorado	22	16	6	3	2.10
1997	Colorado	17	10	7	3	2.21
1998	Colorado	7	3	4	0	2.51
Totals		**160**	**99**	**59**	**11**	**2.38**

Key

GP = Games Played   W = Wins   L = Losses   T = Ties
SO = Shutouts   GAA = Goals-Against Average